EXPERT TELEMARKETING

How to urgently get lots of sales appointments

By Bernard Levine

If you are wanting to fill your diary with lots of sales appointments, this unique book will bring you fast guaranteed results.

Copyright

All rights reserved under International Copyright Law.
No part of this book may be reproduced or transmitted in
any form or by any means, electronic or mechanical,
including photocopying, recording, or by any information
Storage and retrieval system, without the written permission
of the author.
©Bernard Levine 2015

Dedication

To my precious wife, Chrissie thank you so much for all your help and kindness.

To Whiskers (Wikkie) you give me so much joy and fun.

Let's give you what you want!

You urgently need to get quick sales....like yesterday!

You don't have time to waste.

You want to know where to look to find the right people that you can tell them about the services that you have to offer, show them your products and walk away with the signed order.

How do you do it?

You don't want to hear about long explanations of how you should talk on the phone.

You also don't want to be bogged down with lots of boring telephone conversation sales scripts for you to wade through.

What you need right now is the fastest way there is to get to see the people and make the sale.

Okay, let's get on with it!

First and foremost who are you going to talk to?

Have you decided, and do you know who your target market is?

You've got to have an audience to tell your story to and present your product.

Decide who your target market is...what type of companies or buyers do you want to sell to?

Who is most likely to buy your product?

What type of occupation would be most interested in what you have to offer?

Which three specific occupations or professions would be interested in your product or service?

Would it be accountants?... electricians? or engineers?

You must decide and choose who you think would be the most likely type of person who would use your product.

Does your product appeal more to women than to men? Or is it more suitable for children?

Once you have established and decided on a specific target market for your product or service, we can look at where to find the right people you need to approach.

How do you find good leads?

There are so many varied and different places where you can look for prospects to phone.

Have you ever thought of going through the business pages of your local newspaper to see who has been promoted?

Not only will you find the name and job title of the person who has been promoted, but you will also see the name of the company.

Now, all you've got to do is to look up the name of the company in the phone book, or find the company's name on the internet and then phone and congratulate the person who has been promoted.

Everybody likes a warm friendly greeting and your phone call will be welcome and a good way to start your conversation:

'Good morning John. Congratulations on your new appointment!'

An ideal place where you will find names and occupations of key decision makers are at printing shops where they make business cards.

Go along to a few of these printing companies in the area where you work or live, and ask them to show you some examples of their printed business cards.

They will usually bring out a big box of business cards which they have printed for clients.

Search through the many different cards in the box taking careful note of the company's names as well as the job designation of each person's name on the business cards.

(Of course, you should already have a good idea and know the type of company and the occupation of the person you would like to phone).

Ask the printer if you could please have some samples of their business cards. They will gladly give you a whole stack of business cards to take away.

You can also try looking at the classified ads in the newspapers. There, you will find more prospects to phone who could be interested in your products or services.

Referrals are an excellent way to get new clients.

Go along, don't be shy...ask your hairdresser to give you a few contact names and phone numbers of their business contacts, friends and family.

How about asking your next-door neighbour or the people living across the road for some names and numbers...and don't forget to ask your local butcher or convenience store.

Also look for business contact names appearing on signs at super markets and public library notice boards, as well as business cards advertising various services that are left on the counter at your local hardware store.

And don't forget to spend time researching on the web to find the specific categories of the companies you are needing, together with the names of the directors and their contact details.

A good starting point in your telemarketing campaign would be to compile a list of 100 appropriate names for you to contact.

Now, we are going to prepare to start phoning your prospects.

What are you going to say?

What is vital?

The most important point is that we are not going to be selling the product over the phone.

Our only goal and our top priority is to phone and get an appointment.

That's all we've got to do!

When you call, don't give away too much information about what you have to sell them.

Keep them intrigued!

The less they know...the better!

If you tell them too much, you are giving them lots of opportunities to find a reason or an excuse why they should not see you.

Then, you will have to waste time handling their objections.

You are most likely to hear common objections like:

'I can't afford it!', 'I'm not interested', 'I have no use for your product', 'First send me an email, then I'll decide', 'We have already completed our budget' and various other excuses to end the conversation.

Please don't bother and waste time arguing with them and trying to convince them why your product or service is an absolute must-have for them.

It really is not worth it! Just hang up and put the phone down...go forward and move on.

Remember there are hundreds and thousands of other names that you could phone, so why get yourself all in a knot over someone who doesn't even want to give you a chance to even see what your product can do.

Who should you speak to?

Always go straight to the top...

Speak to the decision-makers in the company like the owner, CEO, Managing Director, Financial Director or General Manager. Don't waste your energy and time speaking to the head of the department or a manager...they don't have the power and authority to make a decision.

It depends on what your company is selling ...if you can, try to offer a free trial version of the product or arrange for them to see a demo.

Receptionists have been told by their bosses to screen all calls.

So, how do you get past the receptionist or switchboard operator?

When you call someone, you must not come across or sound like a salesman on the phone.

People are sick and tired of salesmen bothering them.

You've got to have a unique gimmick or a style of your own on the phone.

How you sound and come across in the first 60 seconds of your phone call is absolutely vital.

You've got to set the mood and entertain them.

Be polite, warm and confident.

I am going to give you a secret winning, very unusual telephone approach for you to master....a unique telephone approach that will bring you exceptional success!

It's based on the element of surprise.

The big secret is the receptionist does not expect to receive a phone call like this call that you are about to make....and because it's so very different and not the norm...that's exactly the reason why it works so well!

The receptionist is taken off guard and because she has never received a call like yours before, she does not know how to handle the call.

Remember, you've got to be different and stand out from all the rest of the phone calls that the receptionist receives.

Ring!...Ring!....Ring!

The receptionist answers the phone:

'Good morning Nestle Chocolates....Kathy speaking...How may I direct your call?'

You respond:

'Good morning, I want to speak to that very good looking, adorable, lovable, likeable, intelligent young lady called.....

I didn't get your name.'

(This is very easy to do...it's a mixture of lots of different adjectives that I have put together to fascinate and captivate to grab her attention.

It's even more effective if you practise and say these lines fast...that really gets them going and they like it a lot.)

Why do they like it a lot?

If you think about the daily work and job of the receptionist...every call is usually the same...very routine and mostly very boring.

These are the type of calls the receptionist deals with every day:

'What's the name of your Managing Director? Put me through!'

'Who's in charge of IT department? Put me through!'

The poor receptionist is often abused by the staff at the company and by many of the callers.

At a busy switchboard, the receptionist usually doesn't even get the chance to finish drinking her coffee and often has difficulty in finding someone to take over her duties on the switchboard so that she can quickly go to the toilet.

The way that some of the callers treat the poor receptionist is extremely rude and very bad...

'You cut me off...I'm going to report you! What's your name?'

Now, when the receptionist answers your phone call, it is going to be totally different.

Suddenly, out of the blue comes your phone call, very unusual but so refreshing!

Your phone call is such a welcome break away from all the boring hum-drum phone calls the receptionist gets every day.

The receptionist replies:

'I'm Kathy...who is that? What do you want? Where are you calling from?'

'Hi Kathy, I'm Bernie from Webatar.

Kathy, I need your wisdom, your truth, your love, expertise, professionalism, your help and advice...

Kathy, I need you to hold my hand and point me in the right direction.... please don't squeeze me too hard!'

The receptionist laughs.

'Bernie, you can have everything you've asked for.... how can I help you?'

'Kathy, our company wants to do business with your company....and my boss has asked me to speak to one of your directors or partners to make a short 15 minute to half an hour appointment to see one of your directors.

My boss's name is Malcolm...he wants to find out how you guys operate?... how your company works?... do you charge per hour or per project? so he can know what would be the best way to go forward.'

'Kathy, which director is available now that I can talk to?'

The receptionist answers:

'Okay, I'll put you through to John Royce, he is one of our senior partners...what did you say your name was?... and your company's name?'

'I'm putting you through!'

The director answers:

'Royce, good morning'.

You reply:

'Good morning John Royce. My name is Bernie.

I'm from Webatar. I've been asked to call you by my boss, his name is Malcolm Peterson ….he wants to do business with your company...Malcolm asked me to arrange a short 15 minute to half hour appointment to meet you. The purpose of the meeting is for Malcolm to find out some details such as how you guys operate... and the different services that you offer so he can have a better idea of the way going forward.

John, I don't know if you are a mornings person or an afternoon person?

Would you prefer seeing Malcolm on Tuesday morning, at 10....or would you prefer Wednesday at 2 in the afternoon?

Once you have chosen the day and time you would like,

I'll send you a Microsoft Outlook Invite for you to accept and send back to me.

John, you say you would like to see Malcolm at 10 in the morning on Thursday the 12th July....I'm looking at Malcolm's diary now and I see that he will be available.

Please may I have your email address so I can send you the invite?

Also John, what is your physical address?

Thank you so much John....I'll send you the meeting request now.

Have a good day!

Bye!'

What is important for you to know?

Dial with a smile.

You've got to create the right mood on the phone.

The tone of your voice must be joyful and happy...make them smile or laugh but don't use slang or say anything rude and definitely no dirty jokes...you must not say anything that will offend. Be friendly and polite.

Always give them a choice...let them be able to choose the day and time they prefer...a choice of between one of two different dates.

Telemarketing is a numbers game and the more calls you make, the greater will be your chance of success....

The law of averages will never let you down!

Don't sell your product or service on the phone...you must only focus on getting an appointment.

Book short appointments...time is valuable...long appointments are not welcome and are not appealing.

Make short appointments to get your foot in the door.

Confirm the details of the appointment you have made before you go.

Also confirm the address...search for the company's name on the internet.

There's power in sending a 'thank you' letter after you have been to see the client:

Dear Robert

Just a short note to say 'thank you' for seeing me today.

I really enjoyed talking to you.

I will prepare a new revised quote to send to you tomorrow morning.

Warm Regards

Bernie

What questions should you ask?

There are two different types of questions…open-ended questions and closed-ended questions.

What's the difference between a closed question and an open question?

When you begin your question with any one of the following words, you are asking an open question:

How?

Why?

Where?

When?

Which?

What?

Open questions are good to ask, because it gets them to talk more, explaining and answering in greater detail.

Closed questions will have a short reply of either:

Yes!

No!

Maybe!

Perhaps!

Possible!

If you want a quick short answer, then ask questions that begin with any one of the following words:

Do?

Can?

Could?

Will?

Are?

Should?

May?

Is?

Have?

Would?

Shall?

Did?

Does?

Here are some additional questions you could ask:

'Would you like seeing Malcolm in the beginning of the week or the latter part of the week?'

'Would you rather prefer coming to our offices?'

'What is the name of the product that you are currently using?'

'Which version?'

'What problems are you experiencing?'

'What would you like the product to do for you?'

'Are you involved in the …. industry?'

'Would it help if we could show you a less expensive….?'

'Are you using ….?'

'Have you given thought to the problems you are actually having and the costs you have to incur?'

'How do you deal with….?'

'Is this a problem for your company?'

'Can we give you a solution to meet your budget and requirements? We will save you money and huge costs.'

'Would you like to see a free demo of Webatar?'

'If I can give you..... would you be interested?'

'Are you finding the cost of .....very expensive?'

'Have you ever had to call in a .....to sort out problems you were having?'

SECRETS OF SUCCESS

You are the architect of your life.

Create your own opportunities
and make things happen.

Set yourself a specific goal
and monitor your progress.

Be of service.

Keep doing things for others
without counting the cost.

Turn your defeats into victories.

Control your environment.

Mix with the kind of
people who inspire you.

Keep your attitude positive
and your health in fine trim.

Let God go before you
in everything you do.
Pray regularly with feeling.

Always be planning
something constantly.

You are the magnet of
your circumstances.

Never give up!

In this world, it doesn't matter what people think of you...
the only thing that matters is what God thinks of you.

ALWAYS HAVE A DREAM

Follow your heart
to the path of greatness
that lies within you.

The secret of life
is to have something
to look forward to
every day.

Find a dream that excites you
and make plans
of how you are going
to achieve it.

Feed your mind daily
with positive energy
and words of inspiration.

Take your life to a higher level.

Stay focused and go forward
with your eyes on the prize.

When you run towards your destination
with passion in your heart
you will see your dreams come true.

YOU HOLD THE KEY

Let your determination
be so strong that nothing
can sway its course.

Let your mind believe
so intensely that your dreams
become reality.

Let your actions be rich
with enthusiasm that it moves
the hearts of all.

Let your life be filled
with greater purpose
To reach Higher
To think bigger
To love deeper
than you've ever done before!

www.ingramcontent.com/pod-product-compliance
Lightning Source LLC
Chambersburg PA
CBHW070311190526
45169CB00004B/1587